Renner

CANADA

celebrates multiculturalism

Bobbie Kalman

The Lands, Peoples, and Cultures Series

Crabtree Publishing Company

The Lands, Peoples, and Cultures Series

Created by Bobbie Kalman

For Cynthia Stanko,
a one-woman multicultural celebration

Editor-in-Chief
Bobbie Kalman

Writing team
Bobbie Kalman
Janine Schaub
David Schimpky
Lynda Hale
Tammy Everts

Editors
David Schimpky
Lynda Hale
Tammy Everts

Computer design and layout
Antoinette "Cookie" DeBiasi
Lynda Hale
Campbell Creative Services

Printer
Worzalla Publishing Company

Separations and film
Book Art Inc.

Special thanks to: Caribbean Cultural Committee, City of Nanaimo, Lynn Haliliku, Industry, Science and Technology Canada, Denis Drever and the National Capital Commission, Niagara Grape and Wine Festival, Ontario Black History Society, Oshawa Folk Arts Council, and Tourism Saskatchewan

Photographs

Marc Crabtree: front cover, pages 12-13 (all), 14, 15 (top left, top right, bottom left), 23 (top right, middle right, bottom right), 24
Ken Faris: page 23 (top left)
Industry, Science and Technology Canada: pages 3, 7 (top), 10 (both), 11, 29 (all)
Bobbie Kalman: pages 17 (bottom right), 23 (bottom left), 28
Diane Payton Majumdar: pages 2, 8 (circle), 15 (bottom right)
Tourism Saskatchewan: pages 4-5, 8 (top)

Illustrations

Antoinette "Cookie" DeBiasi: pages 7, 9, 16, 19 (top), 24, 26, 27, 30-31, back cover
Tammy Everts: page 6
Tina Holdcroft: pages 20-21
Maureen Shaugnessy: page 25
Lisa Smith: pages 18, 19
Janet Wilson: page 17 (top)

Published by
Crabtree Publishing Company

350 Fifth Avenue	360 York Road, RR 4,	73 Lime Walk
Suite 3308	Niagara-on-the-Lake,	Headington
New York	Ontario, Canada	Oxford OX3 7AD
N.Y. 10118	L0S 1J0	United Kingdom

Cataloguing in Publication Data

Kalman, Bobbie, 1947-
  Canada celebrates multiculturalism

(Lands, Peoples, and Cultures Series)
Includes index.
ISBN 0-86505-220-4 (library bound) ISBN 0-86505-300-6 (pbk.)
This book looks at the various multicultural celebrations and festivals in Canada.

1. Festivals - Canada - Juvenile literature. 2. Multiculturalism - Canada - Juvenile literature.* I. Title. II. Series.

GT4813.A2K35   1993   j394.2'6

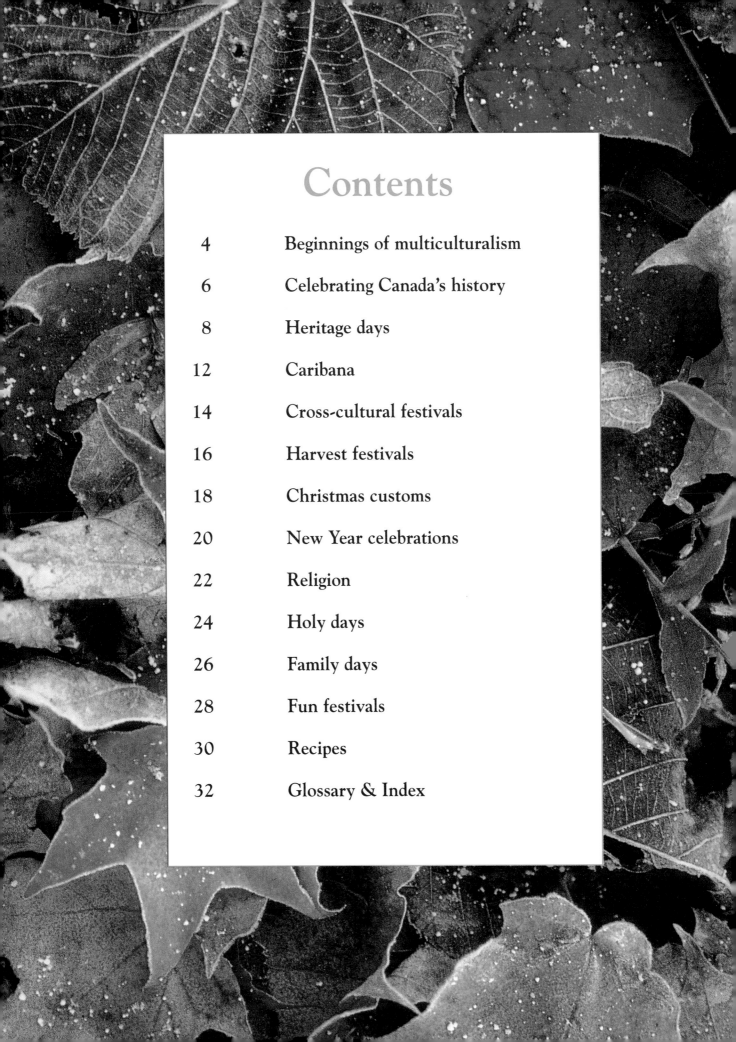

Contents

Native cultures

Canada's first peoples lived on this land more than 4000 years ago. Their cultures and languages were many. When the Europeans came, they changed the lives of the Native peoples forever. Today, Native peoples across Canada are reclaiming their heritage and celebrating their traditional cultures.

French and British

Until the latter part of the nineteenth century, Canada had two main cultural groups: British and French. The majority of the population lived in the eastern part of what is now Canada. By 1885 a railroad was built, which connected the east to the settlements in the west, and Canada's population began to change.

More people came

The Canadian government encouraged American and European farmers to immigrate by offering them cheap land. Thousands of Scandinavian, Belgian, French, German, Polish, and Russian people came. They played an important role in developing the Canadian west.

Over the last 100 years, many more immigrants have made Canada their home. Some came as refugees, fleeing from danger in their countries. Others left their home countries to live in a more prosperous land. Immigrants are attracted by Canada's reputation as a peaceful country.

Celebrating multiculturalism

Canada is a multicultural country. Multicultural means "of many cultures." The different groups in Canada celebrate their old customs and traditions and share in the celebrations of other Canadians. This interesting variety makes Canada an exciting country. Canada is proud of its many peoples. Canada celebrates multiculturalism!

Many cultures can be found in Canada. The people in this picture represent the Native, German, Ukrainian, Filipino, and Indian populations in Canada. Can you identify them by their costumes?

Celebrating Canada's history

Special days are set aside each year to honor certain dates in Canadian history. Some days are times for happy celebrations; others are times for serious reflection. On these "national" days, people across the country think about what it means to be a Canadian.

Canada Day

On July 1, Canadians celebrate their country's birthday. Canada Day, which used to be called Dominion Day, began on July 1, 1867, when the provinces of Ontario, Quebec, Nova Scotia, and New Brunswick united to form one country. The other provinces and territories joined later. Today, people in every part of Canada participate in giant birthday parties that include many different events. In some towns, people share an enormous cake that is baked for this special occasion. In the capital city of Ottawa, choirs sing, bands play, and dancers perform on a huge stage on Parliament Hill. A spectacular fireworks display is broadcast across Canada on television.

Victoria Day

On the Monday before May 25, Canadians remember the birthdays of Queen Victoria and Queen Elizabeth with a sky full of fireworks. This tradition comes from Great Britain, where it was customary to celebrate the monarch's birthday. In Canada, Victoria Day has been a holiday since 1952. On the same day, people in Quebec celebrate Fête de Dollard des Ormeaux. This holiday honors a soldier who was killed in a battle many years ago when Quebec was a French colony.

A rest for workers

Labour Day weekend signals summer's end for many Canadians. It takes place on the first Monday of September and marks the last day of summer vacation for most school children. The day was set aside as an official national holiday in 1894 to honor the hard-working people of Canada who had to endure terrible labor conditions during the nineteenth century.

Remembrance Day

The eleventh hour of the eleventh day of the eleventh month (11:00 am on November 11) is a time to remember. November 11 was originally called Armistice Day because it was the day on which World War I ended. The name was changed to Remembrance Day, and the day became a time to think about the sacrifices made by people in times of war. Canadian war veterans, government officials, and other citizens participate in memorial services. On Remembrance Day, Canadians reflect on how fortunate they are to live in a peaceful country.

(above) On Canada Day, the night sky over Ottawa is filled with the brilliant colors of fireworks.
(opposite page) Weeks before Remembrance Day, people wear red poppies on their jackets and shirts. The poppies represent the flowers that grow in the cemeteries in France and Belgium where many Canadian soldiers are buried.

Remembering a hero

Early in the month of July, people in Saskatchewan celebrate Louis Riel Day. Riel was a Métis leader in the late 1800s. The Métis are people of French and Native heritage. Riel led a rebellion against the Canadian government because settlers were taking over the traditional lands of the Métis. His small army was defeated, and Riel was captured. He was tried and executed for treason in Regina, Saskatchewan. Louis Riel Day is a special day for Native peoples and French Canadians, who remember Riel as a hero.

Louis Riel

Heritage days

What do canoes, rock-lifting contests, fireworks, bagpipes, and Native dances have in common? They are all part of Canada's multicultural heritage! At various festivals across the country, people get together to celebrate their ethnic backgrounds.

The powwow

An ancient custom called the **powwow** is a popular Native gathering. At large powwows, people dress in cultural clothing, eat traditional foods, and buy and sell arts and crafts. The highlight of every powwow, however, is the dancing.

Most of the dances performed at powwows are thousands of years old. The Victory Dance celebrates a successful hunt. The Grass Dance is an ancient warrior dance in which the participants wear grass skirts. In the Fancy Dance, dancers combine fast spinning and twisting with modern dance steps.

During a powwow dancing competition, every detail of the dancer's costume must be perfect. A dancer is disqualified if even one feather or porcupine quill falls to the ground!

Black History Month

Most African Canadians live in Ontario. Various organizations, including the Ontario Black History Society, promote February as Black History Month. Presentations and workshops are held at schools and community centers. Young African Canadians are encouraged to take workshops and participate in activities that teach them about their heritage.

Kwanzaa

In Africa, people celebrate a harvest festival called Kwanzaa, which means "first fruit" in Swahili. Kwanzaa is a time for singing, dancing, and feasting after the harvest. In North America, Kwanzaa is a new holiday that celebrates the culture and history of African Canadians and Americans. An African-American teacher named Maulana Karenga created the modern seven-day festival, which is held just after Christmas.

Some families celebrate Kwanzaa by exchanging gifts, or *zawadi*, visiting one another's homes, and enjoying African-style feasts called *karamus*. On a table in each home is a unity cup, or *kikombe*, filled with water. Every guest who visits during the seven days of Kwanzaa sips from the unity cup to show pride in his or her heritage. The seven days of Kwanzaa represent the Seven Principles, or *nguzo saba*, for living a happy life. These are unity, self-determination, hard work, cooperation, purpose, creativity, and faith. It is very important to people of African heritage that their children learn and follow these principles. On each day of Kwanzaa, a child in the family makes a speech about the virtue for that day and what it means to him or her.

A symbol of pride

At the beginning of the nineteenth century, a famous black leader named Marcus Garvey created a flag called the *bendera*, which had three wide stripes of red, black, and green. Today these colors are used in Kwanzaa decorations such as the *mkeka* or place mat. Red stands for the history of slavery and discrimination against peoples of African origin. Black represents the unity of peoples of African descent. Green means hope for the future of African peoples everywhere.

During Kwanzaa, a candleholder called a **kinara** *is set up in the home. A candle is lit each day, so that by the seventh day of the festival all the candles, called* **mishumaa saba**, *are burning brightly.*

National Ukrainian Festival

At Riding Mountain National Park in Manitoba, thousands of Ukrainian Canadians gather every August to celebrate their heritage with traditional dancing, singing, and feasting. Visitors are warmly greeted and given a piece of bread called *kolach*, which is topped with a lump of salt. According to Ukrainian tradition, bread represents life, and salt adds spice to life.

Fête Nationale

On the night of June 23, fireworks and thousands of bonfires light up Quebec. It is the eve of Fête Nationale. On the next day, the streets are crowded with parades and party-goers. In the past, this grand celebration was held to honor St. Jean-Baptiste (John the Baptist), the patron saint of Quebec. Today this holiday has become a patriotic day on which people in Quebec express their pride in being French Canadian.

Festival du Voyageur

Every winter, people in the town of St. Boniface, Manitoba, celebrate the courage of the voyageurs. The voyageurs were French-Canadian fur traders who journeyed throughout North America by canoe. They were Canada's first business people! Street parties, arts-and-crafts exhibits, and dog-sled races are among the exciting activities at the Festival du Voyageur.

Klondike Days

In 1896, gold was discovered near the Klondike River in the Yukon territory. More than 100,000 people set out from Edmonton, Alberta, to search for gold. The Klondike Days Festival is held in Edmonton each July to commemorate this exciting period in Canada's past. A favorite event is the Sunday parade, in which people dress in nineteenth-century fashions and walk downtown. The buildings are decorated for the parade with false 1890s store fronts. Another event is the Sourdough Raft Race. "Sourdough" was a nickname for an old gold prospector. There is also a contest in which contestants lift rocks and chop logs to determine who is the King of the Klondike.

Oktoberfest

Canada's largest German festival, called Oktoberfest, is held each fall in the Kitchener-Waterloo area of Ontario. People come from near and far to participate in a large parade, dance to the lively music of polka bands, and sample delicious German foods, such as sausages, sauerkraut, and strudel.

Highland Games

Every summer the hills of Nova Scotia come alive with the musical wail of bagpipes. It is the time of year when the Highland Games are held to celebrate the Scottish heritage of Nova Scotia, which means "New Scotland." The cities of Halifax, Antigonish, and Sydney host the largest events. People walk around dressed in Scottish kilts, knee socks, and tams. There are foot races, tug-of-war contests, and Highland dancing. In the caber toss, people compete to see who can throw a heavy pole the farthest. The Highland Games are similar to the celebrations that were once an important part of Scottish life.

Icelandic festival

Gimli, Manitoba, is home to Canada's largest Icelandic-Canadian community. Every year, on the August long weekend, Icelandic Canadians and their friends take part in Islendingadagurinn. What began years ago as a day-long picnic has become a three-day festival of food and fun. This large reunion features rolled pancakes, tug-of-war contests, fireworks, a parade, and a concert. The Viking challenge is a favorite event. It is a pillow fight with a twist—two contestants battle it out while sitting on a pole that stretches over water!

(opposite page, top) **Ukrainian girls greet visitors with kolach,** *their traditional bread.*
(opposite page, bottom) **The fleur-de-lis** *is an ancient French symbol that appears on the flag of Quebec. The name means "flower of the lily." During Fête Nationale, the* **fleur-de-lis** *can be seen on banners, t-shirts, and hats.*
(below) Traditional Scottish outfits worn at the Highland Games include kilts, tams, and knee socks.

Caribana

Caribana is a huge week-long heritage festival that takes place in Toronto each summer. It is based on a yearly carnival that is held on the Caribbean island of Trinidad. The festival originally celebrated the end of slavery in the British colonies in 1834. Toronto's Caribana, which began in 1967, continues the festive tradition. The colorful celebrations include African Canadians and others who came from the Caribbean islands. Caribana invites people of all ethnic backgrounds to join in. Similar celebrations take place in Montreal and Winnipeg. They are called Carifesta and Caripeg.

Floats and bands

The parade is the highlight of Caribana. Floats, crowded with hundreds of passengers dancing to their own traveling band, move slowly along the route. Thousands of people line the streets to watch the happy procession and dance beside the floats.

Long before the festival occurs, the people who are participating in the parade get together to organize their Caribana band. Band leaders must think of a theme for the band, such as "Jamaica's Fruits and Vegetables" or "Sights and Sounds of Trinidad." These themes are called colorful **mas** or fun mas, but there are serious mas, too. A "Water Blues" band might protest the pollution of lakes. A good theme and excellent music are essential if the band wishes to win the "Best-Band" award.

Across the city

Away from the parade route, Caribana is celebrated in many locations. Night clubs, community centers, and even parking lots are alive with reggae and soca music. There is also a two-day picnic on Centre Island in Lake Ontario. People take a ferry to the island to dance, sing, perform, and eat goat-meat roti, Jamaican beef patties, peas and rice, mangoes, and sugar apples.

Caribana participants take months to prepare for **playing mas,** *or taking part in the parade.* **Mas comes from the word "masquerade,"** *a type of party in which people wear disguises. Over 6000 people wear colorful handmade costumes decorated with sequins, sparkles, and shiny material. Some are so enormous that they take up half the street!*

Cross-cultural festivals

The festivals mentioned on the previous pages celebrate the heritage of one particular group of Canadians, such as Ukrainians or African Canadians. There are also hundreds of multicultural festivals held across Canada every year. They feature the folk music, art, storytelling, and dance of many different cultures.

Can you imagine visiting 40 countries in one day? If you visit Folklorama in Winnipeg, Manitoba, or Caravan in Toronto, Ontario, you can do just that! Both Folklorama and Caravan invite visitors to "travel" from country to country. Thousands of people purchase "passports" and visit the international pavilions that are located throughout these cities. Each pavilion offers a chance to discover the traditions, taste the foods, and explore the artistic treasures of a country. Smaller versions of Caravan and Folklorama can be found in cities and towns across Canada.

(above) Toronto's Earth Spirit Festival highlights Chinese, Japanese, and Native cultures.
(opposite page) The Oshawa Folk Arts Council hosts an annual folk festival called Fiesta. Various pavilions display the cultures of Filipino (top left), Caribbean (top right), and Ukrainian (bottom left) Canadians. (bottom right) At the St. Catharines Folk Arts Festival, Miss India poses with a young friend.

Harvest festivals

To the early settlers, harvest time was the most exciting time of the year. Their survival depended on harvesting enough food for the long winter. After the hard work of gathering the crops was over, it was time to celebrate.

A time of thanks

Canadian Thanksgiving is held on the second Monday in October. It is a harvest festival that dates from pioneer days. Some people say that the first Canadian Thanksgiving was held by a French explorer named Samuel de Champlain. Others feel it began as a British festival called Harvest Home. Still other people believe that the Thanksgiving celebration was brought to Canada by settlers who moved north from the United States during the American Revolution.

Canadians and Americans celebrate Thanksgiving in similar ways, but at different times. In both countries, families gather to give thanks for the plentiful food and the joy of sharing it with those they love. Everyone sits down to a traditional meal of turkey, cranberries, potatoes, squash, and pumpkin pie.

Green Corn Festival

In celebration of the upcoming corn harvest, the Iroquois people participate in three days of events to honor the Great Spirit. Throughout the festival, people sing prayers of thanks. During the first two days, participants dance the Great Feather Dance and the Skin Dance of

Mr. Grape is the life of the party at the Niagara Grape and Wine Festival

Thanksgiving. On the third day, the Bowl Game is played. This betting game uses peach stones instead of money, and each player donates clothing to be given away as prizes.

Fairs big and small

A popular form of the harvest festival is the fall fair. Fall fairs are often named after local crops, such as apples, peaches, or cherries. The Eastern Townships Apple Festival in Quebec and the Niagara Grape and Wine Festival in St. Catharines, Ontario, are examples of these festivals.

Other kinds of fall fairs take place across the country. They feature midway rides and games, sideshows, concerts, and other attractions. The largest of these fairs is Toronto's Canadian National Exhibition (CNE). It started long ago as a small agricultural fair for farmers, but today it is the world's largest annual exhibition. It begins in late August and lasts until early September.

Wild Rice Harvest

If you were an Algonquin, Cree, or Ojibwa child living in Manitoba, Saskatchewan, or the northern Great Lakes area of Ontario, you would have two weeks off school in September to help with the wild-rice harvest. Native peoples in these areas gather wild rice, which grows sparsely in shallow lake water. After the harvest, the communities celebrate with a big feast.

Order of Good Cheer

The first European settlers who stayed in Canada were the French. They arrived in the early 1600s and started a settlement called Port Royal in 1605. Port Royal was located in what is now the province of Nova Scotia. It was founded by a French explorer named Samuel de Champlain.

In order to keep his men happy so that they would remain in the New World, Champlain established a club called The Order of Good Cheer. The French settlers at Port Royal took turns hosting great feasts to which they invited the Native chiefs who lived in the area. The host, or Grand Master, served huge platters of venison (deer meat), caribou, moose, beaver, hare, ducks, geese, and all kinds of fish. The Grand Master wore a collar of the Order around his neck and a napkin on his shoulder. With a staff in his hand, he led the other members of the Order, who carried heaping platters of food, into the hall. After eating, the settlers sang, played games, and told stories. Many people feel that Thanksgiving in Canada began with these celebrations.

Harvest moon

Long ago, before electricity was discovered, farmers depended on the large autumn moon to give them enough light to finish harvesting their crops. The Chinese Moon Festival is celebrated when the harvest moon is full. For the Chinese, the moon symbolizes happiness and the cycle of life. To remember this day, Chinese Canadians eat special **mooncakes**, which are round and filled with sweet bean or chestnut fillings.

(below) The Thanksgiving tradition of decorating homes and churches with corn stalks, wheat sheaves, gourds, and flowers has its origins in Harvest Home.

Christmas customs

On December 25, *"Hartelijke Kerstgroeten"* might be the cry you hear in a Dutch-Canadian home. French Canadians greet one another with *"Joyeux Noël."* An Italian Canadian may wish you *"Buon Natale,"* whereas a German Canadian would say *"Fröhliche Weihnachten!"*

"Merry Christmas" is always a happy phrase, no matter what language is spoken. Despite many different customs, Canadians celebrate Christmas with joy and festivity.

Many names for Santa Claus

Most children believe that a man named Santa Claus leaves Christmas presents for them on Christmas morning. People from some cultures, however, call him by different names. Children in Dutch families believe in Sinterklaas who, with his funny helper Black Pete, rides on horseback and delivers presents all night long. French-Canadian children say that Père Noël brings their gifts, whereas German Canadians say that Sankt Nikolaus is the generous bearded man. In some cultures the gift-giver isn't a he—it's a she! Boys and girls in Italian families believe that an old woman named Befana brings presents, but Russian-Canadian children will tell you that it is Grandmother Babushka.

Presents in a bag

Many children hang stockings for Santa Claus to fill, but some boys and girls hang big cloth sacks! Children in British-Canadian families may leave an empty pillowcase tied to the end of their beds. Cree children in northern Canada are fortunate because they leave an empty bag at each relative's house. On Christmas Day, they pick up their bags, which are filled with toys, clothes, and candy!

Christmas in an igloo!

Some Inuit groups meet on Christmas Eve for two days and three nights of church services, contests, games, and feasting. One Christmas many years ago, an Inuit party gathered in a *kaget*, an igloo that was big enough to hold one hundred people! The *kaget* had been specially built for this holiday. Today, the Inuit hold their huge Christmas festivals in community centers and churches.

Newfoundland mumming

Newfoundlanders have an old Christmas tradition called **mumming**. People wrap themselves from head to toe in blankets and old clothes and visit friends and family. The friends they visit try to persuade the mummers to reveal their identities. Eventually, the disguises are removed, and the mummers are invited to share food and drink with their hosts. Canadians in Nova Scotia have a similar custom called **belsnicking**.

Christmas log

In the past, French-Canadian settlers placed special long-burning logs in their fireplaces on Christmas Eve. Later, as fewer people had fireplaces, the tradition changed. Many people kept a symbolic log in their home instead. To continue the log tradition, French Canadians today eat a chocolate "log" cake covered in white icing that resembles snow.

Minuitte

In Quebec, French Canadians celebrate Christmas Eve by attending a midnight church service called *minuitte*. The priest and choir children walk around the church carrying a statue of baby Jesus. After the service, family and friends gather at home to eat traditional meat pies called *tourtières* and sing, dance, and open presents.

(right) Some Italian-Canadian children look forward to the arrival of Befana several days after Christmas. According to an old legend, Befana was too busy to join the Wise Men in bringing gifts to Jesus. Since then, carrying her broom, she leaves presents for all children, hoping that one of them is Jesus. (opposite page) Santa Claus, with his bushy white beard and red outfit, is a familiar sight at Christmas time.

Christmas treats

Candies and desserts are always popular at Christmas. Long ago, people thought that eating sweet things at the end of the year would make the following year a lucky one. Many cultures have different "lucky" treats at Christmas time. French Canadians enjoy a special gingerbread, whereas Scandinavian and German children eat a rich bread called *stollen*. Italian Canadians love a hard, chewy candy called *torrone*. People in eastern Canada may enjoy locally made sweets such as barley candy and chicken bones! Does that sound strange? Chicken bones are actually thin sticks of candy with a chocolate filling.

New Year celebrations

. . . five, four, three, two, one—Happy New Year! Whatever your cultural background, the coming of the new year is an exciting time. It is an opportunity to think about the passing year and wonder what the new one will hold.

Happy New Year

One week after Christmas, Canadians celebrate New Year's Day. Many Canadians welcome the new year by attending parties on the night of December 31. At midnight it is customary to cheer, kiss, and sing the Scottish song "Auld Lang Syne."

In the past few years, Canadian cities have held First Night celebrations on New Year's Eve. These celebrations are for the whole family. Instead of attending parties, people gather in city squares to watch entertainers or take part in singing, dancing, and skating.

Multicultural celebrations

Like Christmas celebrations, New Year festivities vary among the different cultures in Canada. For example, Japanese Canadians eat buckwheat noodles called *soba* that symbolize long life, whereas Portuguese Canadians eat twelve good-luck raisins representing each hour before the stroke of midnight. In Quebec, it is a tradition to visit family and friends on New Year's Eve. Some people collect donations of food, clothes, and money for those who are less fortunate.

Midwinter Festival

For the people of the Iroquois nation, the new year begins five days after the first new moon in January. The Midwinter Festival lasts for eight days. It is marked by wearing traditional clothing, feasting, dancing, and participating in chanting ceremonies.

Chinese New Year

Chinese Canadians celebrate the New Year at the end of January or beginning of February. Chinese New Year is a time to honor ancestors, share a feast with friends and family, and watch dragon and lion dances. The spectacular dragon dance is performed by two people operating a huge papier-mâché dragon head. Twelve more people support the long velvet train. The dragon, which is a symbol of good luck, weaves back and forth to the sound of gongs and drums.

Diwali

Diwali, celebrated in October or November, is a time for Canadian Hindus to worship and rejoice together. Little oil lamps, candles, or electric lights are lit in honor of Lakshmi, the goddess of good fortune, wealth, and happiness. Hindus sometimes call Diwali "the festival of lights" because of the many lamps. Diwali also marks the New Year for many Hindus—a time to pay debts, clean house, and dress in one's best clothes and jewelry.

Rosh Hashanah

The Jewish New Year, called Rosh Hashanah, is held in early autumn. In the morning, families attend a service at the synagogue, where the rabbi blows a ram's horn called a *shofar*. After the service, families enjoy a special holiday meal. It is a tradition to eat a piece of fruit dipped in honey to ensure that the new year will be full of sweet things. Jews look upon Rosh Hashanah as a day to prepare spiritually for the future.

No Ruz

Canadians of Middle-Eastern origin celebrate the new year between March 20 and April 2, depending on the time of the spring **equinox**. The equinox is the time when day and night are equal in length. It occurs once in spring and once in the fall. The festival, called No Ruz, is an occasion for meeting with family and friends. Many rituals are part of the celebrations.

(top) The fierce face of the Chinese New Year dragon is meant to frighten away bad luck!

Religion

Religion is an important part of life in Canada. The Canadian Charter of Rights and Freedoms allows Canadians to practice the religion of their choice. Many immigrants have come to Canada to be able to follow their beliefs. Although the majority of Canadians are Christians, many other religions exist in Canada.

Christianity

Christianity is one of Canada's oldest religions and has the most followers. The first explorers were Christian, as were the missionaries who came to convert the Native peoples. These early French missionaries and settlers were Roman Catholic. The British settlers, who came later, worshipped at the Anglican church. Over the last 150 years, many other kinds of Christian churches have been established in Canada. The United Church is uniquely Canadian. It was formed in 1925 as a union of Methodist, Presbyterian, and Congregationalist churches.

Judaism

Most Canadian Jews follow **rabbinic Judaism**. They meet weekly and hear teachings from a religious teacher called a **rabbi**. Jews believe that God has spoken to people in two ways: through the Scriptures, called the *Torah*, and the teachings of rabbis. Jewish meeting places, called **synagogues**, can be found in most large cities.

Sikhism

The Sikh religion was started in the sixteenth century by a holy man named Guru Nanek who lived in the Punjab region of India. The first Sikhs came to Canada in the early twentieth century and settled in British Columbia. Now Sikh temples, or *gurdwara*, can be found throughout the country. The Sikh religion asks men to practice five outward signs of their faith all starting with the letter "k": long, uncut hair (*kesh*), short pants (*kachha*), a comb (*kangha*), a small dagger (*kirpan*), and a bracelet (*kara*).

Islam

Islam is the religion of Muslims. Most Muslims have come to Canada from North Africa and the Middle East in the last forty years. Canadian Muslims meet in temples called **mosques**. Muslims believe in one God, called Allah, who has revealed himself through a series of prophets. The most important prophet was Mohammed. Mohammed received the Muslim scriptures, called the *Qur'an* (Koran) from Allah.

Buddhism

Japanese immigrants brought Buddhism to Canada. Canadians from other parts of Asia are also Buddhist. They meet in temples to hear Buddha's teachings. The Buddhist religion was started by Gotama Buddha, a teacher who lived in Nepal around 500 BC. Buddhists believe that they live many lives. They practice meditation to experience a feeling of inner peace.

Native religions

Although most Native peoples are Christian, many also believe in their traditional religions. Native religions share several similarities. People worship the Great Spirit who created the universe. Myths and stories explain the cycle of planting and harvest and the relationships among animals, people, and the earth. The **shaman** tells stories and guides the ceremonies.

Hinduism

Hinduism was practiced in India more than 4000 years ago. Hindus believe in one supreme spirit called Brahman. Brahman controls all life and exists as three beings: Brahman the creator, Vishnu the preserver, and Shiva the destroyer. Hindus also believe that a person can have many lives. This cycle of birth, death, and rebirth is called **reincarnation**. Most Canadians who practice Hinduism are of Indian origin.

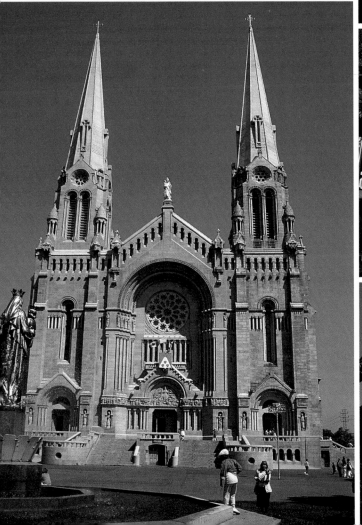

(top left) The inside of this church reflects a mixture of Roman Catholic and Inuit traditions.

(bottom left) Roman Catholics believe that a miracle happened at the site of the Basilica of Sainte Anne-de-Beaupré hundreds of years ago.

(top right) Sikh temples are filled with elaborate decorations and pictures of Guru Nanek.

(middle right) This Buddhist temple displays a **bodhisattva** in front. Buddhists pray to the kind and wise **Bodhisattva** for guidance.

(bottom right) Most Greek Canadians belong to the Greek Orthodox Church.

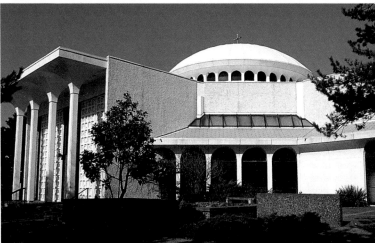

Holy days

Passover

Passover, or *Pesach*, is celebrated by the Jewish community as a festival of freedom. This eight-day holiday is the most important time of the year for Jews! Passover commemorates the escape of the Israelites from slavery in Egypt over 3000 years ago. Families spend weeks studying the *Torah*, cooking, cleaning, and performing charitable acts.

With the first full moon of spring, Passover arrives. On the first night of the festival, the family sits down to a ceremonial meal called the *seder*. Passover foods include *gefilte* fish, *matzah*-ball soup, turkey, green vegetables, horseradish, and hard-boiled eggs. Each of these foods stands for something. For example, green vegetables symbolize spring growth.

The Sun Dance

In Native religions the sun represents the Great Spirit because it helps living things grow and causes seasons to change. The Sun Dance is a prayer to the Great Spirit. By fasting and dancing, Native peoples hope to gain spiritual wisdom. Many of Canada's Native communities have different versions of the Sun Dance. The Iroquois nation holds its Sun Dance in late spring, whereas the Cree have a four-day Sun Dance festival during a full moon in summer.

Saints and souls

Most children celebrate Hallowe'en by wearing costumes and trick-or-treating. Some Canadians, however, spend the last day of October preparing for All Saints' Day and All Souls' Day. On All Saints' Day, held on November 1, some churches hold services to honor the saints who do not have special days of their own. On November 2, Canadians of many cultures celebrate All Souls' Day by visiting cemeteries and placing flowers on the graves of their loved ones. Portuguese and Polish Canadians remember the dead by lighting candles in their honor.

The king of festivals

The twelve-day festival of Rizvan, which is also called the "king of festivals," is the holiest time of the year for Canadians of the Ba'hai faith. It is a time to honor the prophet Baha'u'llah and think about his teachings. The first, ninth, and twelfth days of Rizvan are sacred days on which no one goes to school or work. Instead, the Ba'hai spend their time at prayer gatherings, picnics, and parties.

Birthday of Guru Nanek

In November, Canadian Sikhs gather to celebrate the birthday of Guru Nanek, the founder of their religion. They meet in temples to sing hymns and read their scriptures from beginning to end. The festival, which lasts two days and two nights, finishes with a delicious meal.

(left) *To honor the birthday of Guru Nanek, worshippers set up special altars in Sikh temples.*

Easter

Both Christian and non-Christian Canadians celebrate Easter. Christians observe a religious holiday on Good Friday to remember that Jesus Christ died. They attend a special church service on Easter Sunday to celebrate that he rose from the dead.

Some people think of Easter as a spring festival. For many Canadians, the Easter Bunny has become a part of Easter celebrations. According to tradition, this hopping hare brings eggs and candies on Easter morning. The Ukrainian tradition of painting designs on eggs has become a popular part of this holiday.

A month of prayer

Once a year, Canadian Muslims join other Muslims around the world in a month of prayer called Ramadan. During Ramadan, Muslims do not eat or drink in the daylight hours. This ritual remembers the ancient fast carried out by the prophet Mohammed. Fasting is also meant to remind people of how it feels to be hungry so that they will understand the suffering of those who are less fortunate.

At the end of Ramadan, the fast is broken by a feast called Id-ul-Fitr, "the little festival." After the signal that Ramadan is over, people shout with happiness and pray to Allah.

Easter eggs and rabbits are springtime symbols of birth and life.

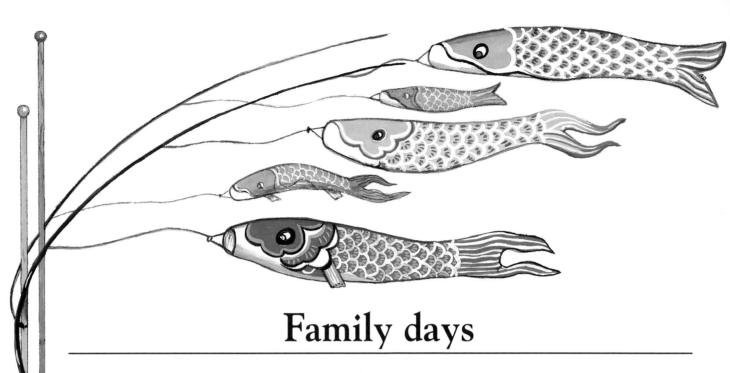

Family days

Many different cultures celebrate their family members on special days throughout the year. In addition to birthdays, days are set aside to honor mothers, fathers, sisters, and brothers. Celebrations often include gifts and a specially prepared meal.

Mother's Day

Thousands of years ago, ancient cultures had holidays to celebrate the mothers of the gods. These celebrations are probably the origin of Mother's Day. In Canada, Mother's Day is the second Sunday of May. In many households mothers are served breakfast in bed or are taken to brunch at a restaurant. Pampering mother with food and gifts is the order of the day!

A day for Dad

The tradition of Father's Day also dates to ancient times. For Canadians, the third Sunday in June has been set aside as Father's Day since 1910. Choosing a gift for fathers is often a challenge for Canadian children; tools and neckties are common presents!

Girls' Day

Girls' Day is an old tradition that celebrates the beauty in nature. It is on the third day of the third month (March 3) and is a special day for Japanese-Canadian girls. The custom in Japan was for each girl to display her collection of ceremonial dolls at her home. Some of these dolls were hundreds of years old. The day was spent visiting the homes of other girls and viewing their doll collections.

Boys' Day

On the fifth day of the fifth month (May 5), traditional Japanese Canadians celebrate Boys' Day. Outside their home, kites shaped like carp fly high in the air. The number of kites used to indicate the number of boys in the family, but today each kite represents one child. In Canada, families of Japanese origin combine Boys' Day and Girls' Day and celebrate the event in early spring by having a party.

(top) Kites, shaped like the carp, fly outside Japanese-Canadian homes on Boy's Day. To lay eggs, carp must swim upriver, fighting the swift current. This fish inspires boys to be just as determined!
(above) Traditional Japanese dolls
*(opposite page) The **tika** ceremony is an important part of many Hindu family celebrations.*

Name Days

Some Christians remember their saints on special days. When children of Christian families are named after saints, their Name Days are celebrated in much the same way as birthdays. In several cultures, Name Days are more important than birthdays! In Greek families, children go to church on their Name Day, and friends bring them gifts just as if it were a birthday. Some names warrant special treatment. For example, if your name is George, everyone who greets you on your Name Day can pull your ears!

Coming of age

Does your culture celebrate a child's passage into adulthood? In the Jewish community the coming of age is a very important event. When Jewish boys are thirteen, a Bar Mitzvah ceremony is held. Girls have a Bat Mitzvah when they turn twelve. To prepare for these ceremonies, boys and girls spend a year learning the Hebrew language and studying the *Torah*, the sacred Hebrew writings. On the day of the Bar or Bat Mitzvah, family and friends are invited to the ceremony in the synagogue. A celebration of feasting, dancing, and fun follows.

Brother and sister days

In the Hindu religion, there are two special days to celebrate brothers and sisters. On the third day of the Diwali festival, brothers and sisters honor one another. In the morning, a sister lights two lamps and marks a *tika* on her brother's forehead. A *tika* is a dot made with red or yellow powder.

In August, Hindus celebrate Raksha Bandhan. A sister buys or makes a bracelet of colored thread or ribbon for her brother. This bracelet, or *rakhi*, is tied around his wrist and confirms that the brother will protect and defend his sister. The sister then puts a *tika* on his forehead. In return, the brother presents gifts or money to his sister. An honorary member of the family can be chosen to perform this ceremony if there is no brother or sister in the family.

Fun festivals

Hallowe'en

When Canadian children dress in costumes and rush from house to house on Hallowe'en crying "Trick or treat!" they are carrying on a tradition that is over a thousand years old. Long ago the Celtic people of Britain and northern Europe celebrated the beginning of their year on October 31 by dressing up in animal skins. The jack o' lantern, a pumpkin carved to look like a head, is an old Irish tradition. Hallowe'en is a favorite time of year for children, who receive plenty of candy and treats when they go trick-or-treating!

Calgary Stampede

In 1912, the famous Calgary Stampede began as "The Greatest Outdoor Show on Earth." The Calgary Stampede Parade opens a ten-day festival of bronco riding, steer wrestling, calf roping, and chuckwagon racing. Over a million people, dressed in cowboy hats, boots, and checked shirts, come to the province of Alberta each July to join in Calgary's biggest and best celebration of the year. Round 'em up, whoa!

Quebec Winter Carnival

The Winter Carnival in Quebec City is a sure cure for the "cooped-up" feeling that Canadians experience in winter. In February, the people of Quebec and thousands of visitors celebrate with ten days of parties, costume balls, parades, and winter sports. People play hockey, toboggan, and take part in dog-sled competitions. Large crowds flock to the edge of the St. Lawrence River to watch the famous ice-boat race. Teams of determined individuals drag, swim, slip, and paddle their small boats over and through the ice floes!

The Quebec Winter Carnival is well known for its ice-sculpture competitions. If you were to walk around the huge carnival ice palace, you might see a snow-sculpted sasquatch, an ice replica of the Eiffel Tower, or a frosty gingerbread house.

Bathtub Race

We usually think of bathtubs as keeping the water *in*, but participants in the annual Bathtub Race, held in Nanaimo, British Columbia, hope that their bathtubs will keep the water *out*! Every July, nearly one hundred motorized fiberglass bathtubs race across Georgia Strait from Nanaimo to Vancouver. Some people come from as far away as Australia to take part in this unusual and exciting event.

Northern sports

Sports and contests have been an important part of Inuit culture for centuries. Traditional games include the High Kick, in which athletes try to kick a ball that hangs down from a tall pole. A game called *ajaraq* is a tug-of-war, but the two contestants pull with their heads instead of their hands! These sports are played at a festival called Toonik Tyme, which takes place in the northern town of Iqaluit. Other less traditional activities include human sled races, the backwards parka race, and a broomball game in which participants wear a shoe on one foot and a skate on the other. Another occasion for traditional Inuit competitions is the Arctic Winter Games. More familiar winter sports, such as cross-country skiing and curling, are part of these games.

(above) Jack o' lanterns, costumes, and candy make Hallowe'en lots of fun.

(above) That's using
your head! These men
are competing in a
game of **ajaraq**.
(below) The chuck-
wagon races are an
exciting part of the
Calgary Stampede.

(middle) The symbol
of the Quebec Winter
Carnival is Bonhomme,
a snowman who wears
a red toque and sash.
He lives in the ice
palace—a huge
structure made of ice!

Recipes

Canada is a land of many cultures. As a result, Canadians enjoy a wide variety of cultural foods. In an Inuit home, you might sit down to a hearty meal of caribou steak, a dish of delicate white fish called arctic char, or a nutty-tasting mouthful of whale blubber called *muktuk*. Plump perogies would be a delicious part of dinner with a Ukrainian family on the prairies. A French-Canadian meal might include *poutine*—french fries topped with melted cheese and gravy. If you want a taste of Canada, try some of these recipes. Make sure you have an adult with you when you use a knife, blender, oven, or stove.

Quebec Pea Soup

Pea soup is a very old tradition in Quebec. It was eaten by the *habitants*, Quebec's early settlers. It is especially welcome on a cold winter day!

550 g (1 1/4 pounds) dried green peas
225 g (1/2 pound) salt pork
2.5 liters (11 cups) water
120 ml (1/2 cup) chopped celery
60 ml (1/4 cup) chopped parsley
2 diced onions
3 bay leaves
5 ml (1 teaspoon) pepper
5 ml (1 teaspoon) savory

Wash and drain peas and put them in a soup pot. Boil for two minutes. Remove from heat and let cool for two hours. Add rest of ingredients. Bring soup to a boil again, then turn down heat and let simmer for two hours.

Bannock

The Native peoples were the first to make bannock. They baked this dough over an open fire. When Europeans came to Canada, they changed the recipe and fried bannock in a pan. This is a modern version of this classic Canadian bread.

500 ml (2 cups) flour
500 ml (2 cups) water
pinch of salt
15 ml (1 tablespoon) baking powder
1 egg
15 ml (1 tablespoon) sugar
lard or vegetable oil

Mix flour, water, salt, and baking powder in large bowl. Add egg and sugar. Ask an adult to fry the bannock for you. Heat frying pan at medium high and add oil or melt a spoonful of lard. Pour one-third of bannock mixture into pan and cook until small bubbles appear. Add a bit more oil, flip bannock over, and cook until second side is done. Cut into pieces and serve warm. This recipe makes three bannock rounds. Try bannock with Quebec Pea Soup, spread jam on top, or enjoy it on its own.

Sesame Spinach Salad

This simple Japanese salad calls for two ingredients often used in Japanese cooking: sesame seeds and soy sauce. This dish can be prepared quickly. You will love it!

1 bag or bunch of fresh spinach
90 ml (6 tablespoons) sesame seeds
25 ml (5 teaspoons) sugar
60 ml (4 tablespoons) soy sauce
60 ml (4 tablespoons) chicken bouillon or water

Remove spinach stalks, rinse spinach, and drain in a colander. Pour hot tap water over spinach. Leave to drain. Roast sesame seeds under the broiler until light brown. Spread out on a cold plate to cool. In a bowl, combine seeds, sugar, soy sauce, and bouillon. Stir until sugar dissolves. Beat well with a small whisk. Put drained spinach in a bowl. Pour dressing over spinach carefully to cover all the leaves.

Yogurt and Cucumber

This recipe is part of the cuisine of many different countries. The spices are different, but the result is much the same. Hungarians use sour cream instead of yogurt, and they spice the cucumbers with paprika. Greeks use lots of garlic. The Lebanese add mint instead of ginger root. This recipe is South Asian. It goes well with the curry dish on this page. If your mouth gets too hot from the curry, you can soothe it with a cool mouthful of yogurt and cucumber.

1 large cucumber
7.5 ml (1/2 tablespoon) salt
150 ml (2/3 cup) plain yogurt
1 crushed garlic clove
2.5 ml (1/2 teaspoon) grated ginger root
7.5 ml (1/2 tablespoon) lemon juice

Grate cucumber and season with salt. Leave cucumber to drain in a strainer for one hour. Mix together yogurt, garlic, ginger, and lemon juice. Just before serving, pour yogurt mixture over the cucumber and stir gently.

Vegetable Curry

Many exotic spices are combined to make curry. This tasty seasoning has its origins in Indian food. Curry is also the name used for dishes that are heavily spiced with curry. Curries are usually served with rice.

550 g (1 1/4 pounds) green beans
3 large ripe tomatoes
15 ml (1 tablespoon) butter
1 medium onion, chopped
5 ml (1 teaspoon) grated ginger root
10 ml (2 teaspoons) curry powder
60 ml (1/4 cup) water
pinch of salt
few drops of lemon or lime juice

Trim beans and slice each into three pieces. Cut tomatoes into small chunks. Heat butter and stir-fry onion until transparent. Stir in ginger root and fry for 30 seconds. Mix in curry powder and tomato pieces. Add beans, water, and a little salt. Bring mixture to a boil. Reduce heat and partially cover the saucepan. Cook at low heat for 8 to 10 minutes. Before serving, add a few drops of lemon or lime juice.

Banana Punch

This refreshing tropical recipe serves 20 thirsty friends.

1 large can pineapple juice
375 ml (1 1/2 cups) orange juice
60 ml (1/4 cup) lemon juice
3 large bananas mashed or pureed in blender with some juice
1 liter (36 ounces) ginger ale

Mix together juices and banana. Decorate with cherries and orange, lemon, and banana slices. Just before guests arrive, add some ice cubes. Pour in ginger ale to make the punch sing!

Glossary

blubber The layer of fat on some marine mammals, such as whales and seals

bronco A wild male horse

caribou A large member of the deer family that lives in the northern part of Canada and Alaska

chuckwagon A wagon used for carrying food and supplies for cowboys

ethnic Describing or relating to a social group connected by heritage, language, or race

fast The practice of not eating for a period of time

fiberglass A light material made from small threads of glass

gefilte **fish** Fish mixed with bread crumbs and eggs

Hebrew The ancient language of the Jews

hymn A religious song

immigrant Someone who settles in a new country

mas From the word "masquerade," a type of party in which people wear disguises

matzah **ball** A dumpling made from unleavened bread that is eaten during Passover

meditation Sitting quietly with one's eyes closed so that the mind can rest

missionary Someone who goes to a different country to spread religious beliefs

monarch The ruler of a country who has inherited his or her throne

myth A traditional story that tells the beliefs of a group of people

pavilion A temporary structure used at a fair or festival or a building used for a celebration at a cross-cultural event

prophet A person who is believed to speak on behalf of God

refugee A person who moves to a new country because of danger in his or her home country

roti A meat-filled soft bread

sasquatch A legendary ape-like creature

Scandinavian Describing the inhabitants of Denmark, Sweden, and Norway

shaman A religious leader believed to have special powers

soca music Improvised songs, originally from the island of Trinidad

treason The crime of betraying one's country

Index

1 2 3 4 5 6 7 8 9 0 Printed in U.S.A. 2 1 0 9 8 7 6 5 4 3